Dedicated to my ʻaumakua Honu,
who guides me both in and out of the ocean.
Aloha from your hānai daughter, Palapala

Mahalo nui loa to those who give freely of their time,
creative energy and expertise.

Nan Hee Berg ~ Layout
John Kiah Berg ~ Technical Support
Skippy Hau ~ Hawaiian Honu Expertise
Ipolani Medeiros ~ Hawaiian Text
Michael Napier ~ Technical Support
Scott Wenham ~ Photographer
Pacific Printing & Publishing
And all my other helpers.

HAWAIIAN ALPHABET

LONG

ā as in father	**ō as in rose**
ē as in obey	ū as in rule
ī as in marina	

SHORT

â as in art	**ô as in low**
ê as in egg	û as in pull
î as in igloo	

Consonants

' (okina) in English = glottal stop

h, k, l, m, n, p, w ~ pronunciation as in English,

except: "w" ranges soft "w" + soft "v"

Also by Barbara E. Berg

Honu The Green Sea Turtle

Pacific Printing & Publishing, Honolulu, Hawaii
ISBN: 0-9729118-2-0

Alohahonu

Barbara E. Berg

Alohahonu looks around the
bay for something to do.

**ʻImi ʻo Alohahonu
i kekahi hana i ke kai kūʻono.**

1

Some honu are surfing the waves.
Alohahonu surfs too.

Ke heʻenalu nei kekahi mau honu.
Heʻenalu pū ʻo Alohahonu.

2

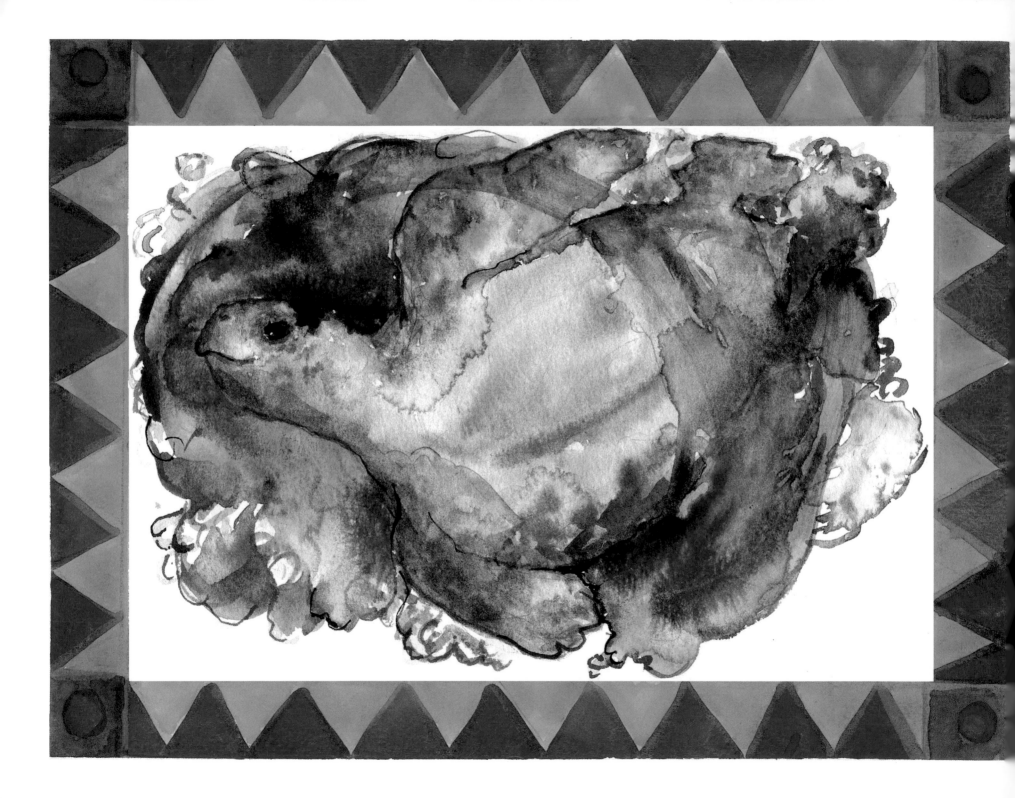

Alohahonu has fun rolling
in the waves.

**Nui ko Alohahonu leʻaleʻa i ke
kakaʻa ʻana i ka nalu.**

3

Alohahonu and a friend
dive down for some seaweed.

**Lu'u iho 'o Alohahonu
a me kona mau hoaaloha i ka limu.**

4

This is very good seaweed and Alohahonu feels happy.

ʻOno loa ka limu a hauʻoli ʻo Alohahonu.

5

Alohahonu
goes by the grooming station,
but decides to be groomed later.

**ʻAu ʻo Alohahonu
i kahi hoʻonaninani
akā ʻaʻole ʻo ia i makemake.**

6

Alohahonu sees a
spinner dolphin friend.

**'Ike 'o Alohahonu
i kona hoaaloha ka nai'a.**

7

Some dolphins are playing keep-a-way with a noni leaf.

Ke pā'ani ho'omamao nei kekahi mau nai'a me ka lau noni.

8

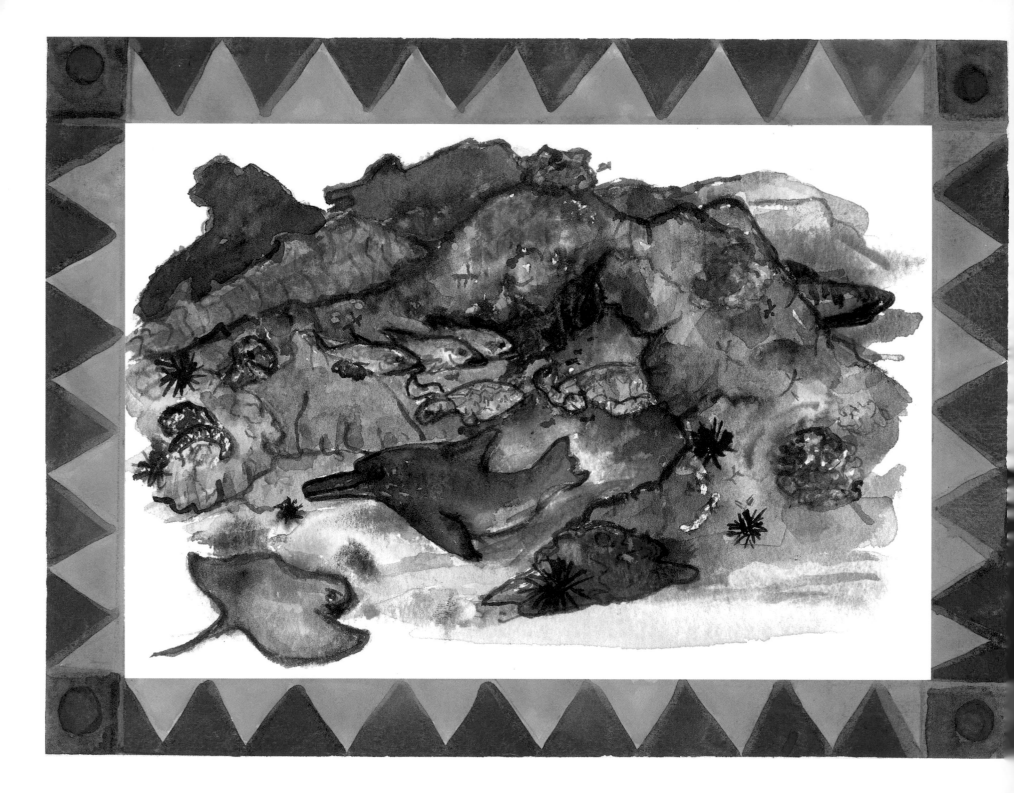

Alohahonu and friends go through an archway into the bay nearby.

'Au 'o Alohahonu a me kona mau hoaaloha i ka hoaka o ke kai kū'ono kōkoke.

9

A big honu is tied up in fishing line and can barely get to the ocean surface to breathe.

Pa'a 'ia kekahi honu nui i ke aho a 'a'ole hiki iā ia ke 'au i ka 'ilikai e hanu ea.

Alohahonu and the friends
cannot free the big honu
from the fishing line.

**ʻAʻole hiki iā Alohahonu a me
kona mau hoaaloha ke hoʻokuʻu
i ka honu nui mai ke aho.**

11

They return to their bay and Alohahonu takes a nap. A peacock flounder tries to camouflage itself on the turtle's shell as three eagle rays glide above.

Hoʻi lākou i ko lākou kai kūʻono ponoʻi i ka hiamoe iki. I ke ʻau ʻana o ʻekolu hailepo i luna, ʻau ka pakiʻi a hoʻopeʻepeʻe ma luna o ke una o ka honu.

Alohahonu dreams.
A little mermaid visits and finds out
that a big honu is in trouble.

Moe'ūhane 'o Alohahonu.
Kipa mai kekahi wahine hi'u i'a a 'ike
'o ia he pilikia ko honu nui.

13

A zebra moray eel shows the little mermaid a shortcut to the nearby bay.

Hōʻike ʻo puhi iā wahine hiʻu iʻa i ke ala ʻoki i ke kai kūʻono kōkoke.

Pearly tears drop from the
mermaid's eyes.

**Kulu waimaka momi mai nā maka
o wahine hiʻu iʻa.**

A piece of lava rock helps to
cut the fishing line.

'Oki 'ia ke aho i ka 'āpana 'a'ā.

16

The happy big honu swims away.

'Au aku ka honu nui hau'oli.

17

Alohahonu and friends
wave goodbye.

**Peʻahi lima ʻo Alohahonu a me
kona mau hoaaloha,
A Hui Hou Aku Nō.**

18

Do you want to help Honu and friends? When you go into the ocean to visit the honu, please do not chase the sea creatures. Honu will come to you. Touch only with your eyes. Take nothing away from Honu's home, except debris left by other people. Never feed wild creatures, this interferes with their food chain and the balance of nature. Avoid polluting the water by wearing a rash guard or t-shirt to protect your skin. Defog your mask with baby shampoo or a natural toothpaste. Have fun and take someone with you.

Honu has led me to some new friends ~ the spinner dolphins. Let me know if you want to know more about them and other sea creatures.

Barbara E. Berg
www.alohahonu.com
barbara@alohahonu.com
P.O. Box 959
PMB 625
Kihei, HI 96753-0959

Glossary

Green Sea Turtle ~ **Honu**

The sea turtle has inhabited the earth for 180,000,000 years. The honu is a reptile and needs air to breathe. Green sea turtles eat sea plants. The honu reproduces by laying eggs in sandy nests onshore. The hatchlings are on their own once they crawl to the sea and only about 1 in 10,000 reach maturity. The honu can live to 80 years and grow to be 400 pounds. The green sea turtle is an endangered species in Hawaii.

I

Photo © 2004 Scott Wenham

Glossary

Mermaid ~ Wahine hiʻu iʻa

The mermaid is a legendary sea creature with the head and trunk of a beautiful girl or woman and the tail of a fish. More about the mer people will be in a book soon to be available.